7051204 | VINCENT, K. £5.50 | NAILSEA GLASS

748.292

NAILSEA GLASS

One of a pair of carafes (see plate 34).

NAILSEA GLASS

KEITH VINCENT

DAVID & CHARLES
Newton Abbot London
North Pomfret (Vt) Vancouver

Dedicated to the memory
of Nailsea's craftsmen
glassblowers

0 7153 6807 9

Set in 11 on 13pt Imprint and printed in
Great Britain by Redwood Burn Limited, Trowbridge & Esher
for David & Charles (Holdings) Limited
South Devon House Newton Abbot Devon

Published in the United States of America
by David & Charles Inc North Pomfret
Vermont 05053   USA

Published in Canada by Douglas, David &
Charles Limited 3645 McKechnie Drive
West Vancouver BC

CONTENTS

1 HISTORY 1788 - 1873

John Robert Lucas, 1754-1828, who founded the Nailsea Crown Glass and Bottle Manufacturers in 1788, by W. A. Hobday RA, 17? *(Courtesy of Bristol City Art Gallery)*

In 1788 a glasshouse, consisting of a cone and a single furnace, was built at Nailsea, in Somerset, for the manufacture of crown window glass. Nailsea was then a small village, situated between Bristol and Clevedon, with useful supplies of coal, limestone and sand nearby. Together with a rented glasshouse at nearby Stanton Wick and a warehouse and counting-house in Nicholas Street, Bristol, the new glasshouse was the premises of the newly formed company known as the Nailsea Crown Glass and Bottle Manufacturers. The man solely responsible for this venture was John Robert Lucas. Born in 1754 and originally a hooper, he was until 1788 primarily concerned with the marketing of beer and cider and of bottles in the Bristol area. A notice dated 28 July 1788 appeared in the *Bristol Gazette* on 14 August announcing Lucas's intention to confine himself solely to the Crown Glass and Bottle Manufactures and of his wish to dispose of the beer and cider business which he had carried on for many years in Nicholas Street.

His furnaces subsequently produced not only window glass and bottles, but sometimes also individual pieces like flasks, rolling-pins, jugs, top hats and walking-sticks, sometimes decorated with flecks, loops or bands of white or coloured enamel.

No doubt Lucas, whose portrait by W. A. Hobday is in the Bristol City Art Gallery, would have been surprised to learn that the name Nailsea would later be used, long after the closure of the works there, to describe a great deal of domestic and fancy glass, much of which had not even been made there; and that Nailsea glass would be keenly sought after by collectors for private and museum collections both in Britain and abroad, including the USA.

The Nailsea story has the seeds of its origins much further back in time than the eighteenth century – ultimately to the time when glass vessels were first made in Ancient Egypt. The continuity of the art and craft of glassmaking can be seen in the similarities between the combed and threaded decoration used by both Egyptian and Nailsea craftsmen. Further reference will be made to early foreign influences later on.

Glasshouses were established in Bristol during the seventeenth century. In the course of the next century, glassmaking became a very important industry, window glass and bottles being its mainstay and of renowned quality. R. Neve's *Builders Dictionary* of 1703 stated that Bristol window glass was better than most. John Robert Lucas was a partner in the Limekiln Glasshouse, where bottles were made, until 1793.

Coloured flint glass of fine quality was also made in Bristol and this city has given its name to that type of glass in rich and deep shades of green, blue and amethyst which was also made elsewhere. Some of this fine glass was decorated in the Nailsea style (see plate 28). Fine white enamel glass resembling porcelain was also made there and is likely to have been the source of supply for the white flecks, loops and bands which embellish much of the Nailsea country ware.

Production of flint glass was hampered by the excise duty introduced in 1745 and ever on the increase until 1845. It has often been suggested that this duty was the catalyst for the establishment of the Nailsea enterprise for the specific manufacture there of domestic and table ware in the much less taxed window and bottle glass, decorated to make it more attractive to the eye. Far more likely is that an increasing demand for window glass, or Lucas's anticipation of it in an age of industrial progress and expansion, was responsible. Records and other evidence prove the point.

In 1790 a second crown glass furnace was erected. William Chance and Edward Homer, hardware merchants from Birmingham, became partners in 1793, strengthening the business financially. Each of them married sisters of Lucas. William Coathupe was the fourth partner. A bottle house was acquired by the firm in Bristol in 1806, but the extent and period of manufacture is not known. Bottles were also made at the rented works at Stanton Wick until the lease was terminated in 1815. Bottles were made at Nailsea, perhaps from this time, and a plan of 1870, in the possession of Chance Brothers, shows the site of an old bottle house. It is not really known for how long bottles were made, but records suggest that production had ceased by the 1830s, at the latest.

Robert Lucas Chance, eldest son of the aforementioned William, and Lucas's nephew, became the manager at Nailsea in 1811, when he was twenty-nine years of age. An extremely shrewd and able young man, who had already managed the family hardware business at the age of fourteen, he spent four years at Nailsea. During this time he improved the efficiency of the management of the business and learnt the manufacturing processes – experience that was to stand him in good stead in 1824, when he bought the British Crown Glass Company at Smethwick, near Birmingham, and so founded the enterprise of Chance Brothers, which was to acquire the Nailsea works for the last three years of its operations, and which is still in existence today. He left Nailsea in 1815, sold his shares and became a glass merchant in London.

During his managership he had acquired the services of John Hartley, of Dumbarton, by reputation the leading crown glass technologist in the country, and so highly did he value his expertise that when Hartley's Nailsea contract expired in 1828 he engaged him for his Birmingham business. In this same year John Robert Lucas died. John Hartley died in 1833 and in 1836 his two sons founded the firm of Hartley's of Sunderland which was later to acquire the Nailsea freehold for a short time before Chance Brothers finally took it over in 1870.

Window glass was the main concern at Nailsea, but the heavy excise duty on flint glass could have stimulated the production of domestic ware from both crown and bottle glass as a sideline. A large variety of useful domestic wares were traditional products to use up pot remains at the end of a shift or journey and useful articles were often catalogued by window glass factories in the nineteenth century. In an article in *The Connoisseur*, Sir Hugh Chance refers to a list of such articles made by Chance Brothers at Smethwick in 1868. It includes preserve jars, propagating glasses, ships' lights, milk pans, pastry pans, fern stands, bee glasses, fish globes, aquaria, rolling-pins, cucumber frames and gauge tubes.

The Napoleonic Wars could have endangered shipments of crown glass to Ireland and elsewhere and this could have been a further incentive. Bristol customs records, Presentments, which give details of exports from the port of Bristol, show that the main products were window glass and bottles. A sample analysis made for January and February 1790 shows that well over 50,000 bottles, most of them empty, and approaching 200 sides of window glass were exported to destinations like Cork, Waterford, Newry, Jamaica, New York and Philadelphia. An interesting entry during this period records that under the name of J. R. Lucas ten casks of beer and cider were shipped in the *Pearl*, John Wilding master, bound for Africa. This was over two years after Lucas's declared intention to confine himself solely to the manufacture of crown glass and bottles. Other firms exporting window glass and bottles to similar destinations were Ricketts, Elton Miles & Company and Virgo Stevens. In a corresponding two-month period in 1825, Lucas, Coathupe & Company exported 600cwt of crown window glass to Cork, Waterford, Dublin, Tobago, New York and Philadelphia.

Considerable gaps in the records of the Nailsea enterprise, particularly for the early years of the nineteenth century, obscure what had actually been made there besides crown window glass. Abstracts of balance and accounts for the period between 1807 and 1828 were in the possession of a descendant of J. R. Lucas prior to the last war, but they were sent to Plymouth for storage after the outbreak of hostilities and were lost in the heavy blitz on that city. The late H. St George Gray, Curator of the Castle Museum, Taunton, from 1901 to 1949, had

access to these for research purposes at one time, but unfortunately he made no written record of their contents, although they are mentioned in the last of three of his articles on Nailsea glass in *The Connoisseur*.

By 1835 the Nailsea glassworks was considered to be one of the four most important window glass factories in England. An interesting works notebook kept by C. J. Coathupe, the manager, in 1836–7 was discovered in a private safe at Chance Brothers, Birmingham, by Sir Hugh Chance before the war. It is important to note that it is solely concerned with window glass and alkali manufacture and it appears to give a picture of the whole of the firm's operations at Nailsea during this time including the detailed recipes for making two similar kinds of glasses. At this time the firm's business paper was headed Lucas, Coathupe and Co, Crown Window Glass and Alcalis and there is an example of a receipt so headed in the City Art Gallery, Bristol (plate 1).

Could flint and enamel glasses have been manufactured at Nailsea at the same time? For technical reasons Sir Hugh Chance discounts this suggestion. In his paper 'Nailsea Glass' he says:

> Bristol enamel (and also flint) glass has a very high lead content requiring a much lower temperature in melting than crown or bottle glass. Crown sheet and bottle glass is melted in open pots; glass containing a high content of lead oxide is melted in covered pots to avoid reduction of lead oxide into metallic lead by furnace gas action. It would not be economic to operate open and closed pots in the same furnace.

And during the period of the excise duty on glass an excise officer always had to be on duty during operations. One of his duties was

1 The head of a receipt, dated 12 September 1837, in the name of Lucas, Coathupe & Company, the firm's title at that time, but one of a number of titles, which changed from time to time during the firm's history.

to see that only one type of glass was melted in one glasshouse.

The manufacture of sheet glass was commenced in 1844 and a period of expansion began in 1845 helped by the removal of the window tax and excise duty. In 1851 the construction of Joseph Paxton's Crystal Palace for the Great Exhibition heralded a new age of glass. The Nailsea firm had tendered for this prestigious contract, but it went to Chance Brothers. In 1855 the rights were sold to Isaac White. They were leased to Samuel Bowen and John Powis in 1862. In 1865

2 The Nailsea Glassworks. Cone supports, revealed during demolition works in 1905. The works finally closed in 1873.

3 The Nailsea Glassworks. This photograph, taken by Sir Hugh Chance about 1930, shows the row of glassworkers' cottages, beyond the ruined wall of the glasshouse. The scene looks much the same today, only the rubble has been removed, the wall has been tidied up and still forms the boundary between the field and the cottage gardens.

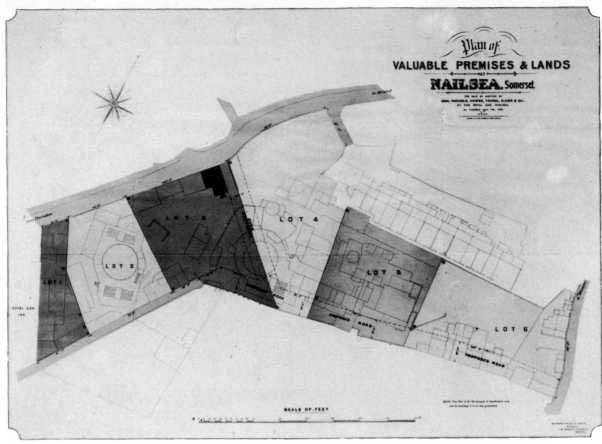

there were two sheet glasshouses and one rolled plate house. In the sixties large quantities of rolled plate glass were consigned to Crewe and other large railway stations. By this time the manufacture of crown glass had ceased. Coloured flashed sheet glass, and brilliant cut was also produced. The freehold was sold to Hartley's of Sunderland in 1869. In 1870 it was bought by Chance Brothers, who manufactured sheet and rolled plate cathedral glass. Just three years later came the closure. The local coal supply at Nailsea Heath had deteriorated in quality, resulting in the production of an inferior glass and a consequent accumulation of stock. Much of the works was demolished in 1905, what remained gradually becoming more overgrown and ruinous. The buildings that have survived have been converted to other uses and there are still a few ruins and a wall which backs on to the gardens of a row of cottages, Whitcombe's Rank, now known as Woodview Terrace. Fragments of window glass may be found here and I was given recently two pieces by a cottager, Mrs Nicholson, née Garland, whose great uncle of this name had been employed at the glassworks. The cottages known as French Rank have been demolished and replaced by council flats.

4 The Nailsea Glassworks. This plan of 1905 shows the site of the glassworks. To the north of lots 4, 5 and 6 is the row of cottages built by Lucas for his employees and known as Whitcombe's Rank. In the gardens of these cottages, fragments of glass, of various hues of pale green, are occasionally found.

2 THE GLASSMAKERS

What do we know of the men who made the glass? Families with a history of some generations' residence in the district often have interesting information and pieces of glass, perhaps made by their ancestors, which have been handed down from generation to generation. Such information can often help us to discover or confirm what was made at a particular time. On a recent visit to Nailsea I learnt from the Brocks of Laurel Farm, adjacent to where the glassworks once stood, that an ancestor of theirs, Peter Dodds, worked there. They showed me his marriage certificate of 1863, which described him as a glassblower, and a piece of ruby flashed sheet glass which had been brilliant cut to reveal a heart and border decoration with the initials WS, AR and a P which the family thought had been given to the bridegroom to commemorate his wedding. Sheet glass, flashed in red, blue and orange, was made in the sixties at Nailsea according to a pattern sheet with the heading, 'The Nailsea and Stourbridge Glass Company', with leaf and floral designs which could be cut to order. I was shown a piece of dark blue ribbed undulating/interlocking glass which was advertised by the firm in the sixties; a piece of similar design in pale green glass is in the Bristol City Art Gallery (see plate 55). Mrs Patricia Elton of Clevedon Court has a piece of flashed ruby glass, cut in an elaborate floral pattern. I was also able to compare from these sources two kaleidoscopes, one containing fragments of coloured glass in blue, red, green, orange and clear glass and the other with the same colours and a paler green and pink as well.

To return to the early days of the enterprise's history, a notice in the *Bristol Gazette* of 19 August 1790 concerns four runaway apprentices, namely, Joseph Dully, Robert Warren, Nathaniel Warren and William Smart, apprentices to John Robert Lucas of Bristol, who absconded from the Glass Bottle Manufactory of Lucas, Pater and Coathupe at Stanton Wick. Notice was given that any person harbouring or employing them would be prosecuted most severely. Detailed descriptions of the runaways are given, followed by a notice of a £2 2s 0d reward for their apprehension.

Hannah More, a pioneer Christian social worker, with her sister Patty More founded fifteen Sunday Schools in the Bristol area at the end of the eighteenth century and they visited Nailsea on 30 September 1791 to lay the foundation stone of the Nailsea Sunday School.

September 30 1791. With a humble reliance on the blessing of Almighty God, this little building was begun with a sincere desire to promote His Glory, to benefit the parish of Nailsea in its most important interest, the education of the rising generation in the knowledge of the Christian religion.

Of her contacts with the glassworkers she wrote:

. . . we now made our appearance for the first time among the glasshouse people, and entered nineteen houses in a row (little hovels) containing in all near two hundred people. The work of a glasshouse is an irregular thing, uncertain whether by day or night; not only infringing upon man's rest, but constantly intruding upon the Sabbath. The wages high, the eating and drinking luxurious, the body scarcely covered but fed with dainties. The high buildings of the glasshouses ranged before the doors of these cottages – the great furnaces roaring – the swearing, eating and drinking of these half dressed black looking beings – gave it the most horrible appearance. One if not two joints of finest meat were roasting in each of these hot little kitchens, pots of ale standing about and plenty of early looking vegetables. We were in our usual luck respecting personal civility, which we received from even the worse of these creatures, some welcoming us to 'Botany Bay', others to 'Little Hell' as they themselves shockingly called it. We talked to them a great deal and indeed they all listened, some with great delight and attention.

Another account appears in Patty More's journal, taken from *The Life of Hannah More*:

Nailsea: we made our appearance here for the first time and entered nineteen little hovels in a row, containing in all near two hundred people. We had already encountered savages, hard hearted farmers, little cold country gentry, a supercilious corporation; yet this was unlike all other things, not only different, but greatly transcending all we had imagined. We had a gentleman with us, who personally being rather fearful, left us to pursue our own devices, which we did by entering and haranguing every separate family. We obtained the promise of twenty-seven children. The colliers even are more like human beings than the people of the glasshouses.

There was a Nailsea Glassworkers Guild, which held its meetings at the Glassmakers Arms (now the Friendship Inn). The Guild possessed two glass pole heads which represented the insignia of the Guild (pole heads were traditionally carried by village clubs in Somerset and border parishes and made of brass and sometimes wood, iron and nickel plate). In the glassworks' heyday there were twenty-six pubs in the village and fights were common. Whether this belligerence was affected by the efforts of the sisters More is debatable, but the sisters claimed that the 'savage' glassworkers had been considerably tamed by the end of the century! However, the problems that they tried to alleviate were still apparent seventy years later when the Children's Employment Commission was making its investigations in the area in 1865. The investigator stated that the glassworks were 'peculiar' in that they were in an entirely country district and that the boys, who arrived before the blowers for work, looked healthy, more so than in other glasshouses. Verbatim accounts from Samuel Bowen, manager, and from two of the youths employed follow. Of 200 employees fifty were under the age of eighteen. The boys would work a thirteen- or fourteen-hour shift or 'journey', their duties being to push sheet cylinders into the kilns and to gather glass on the pipes before the blowers arrived to make the irons fit for use. The youngest, of about eleven to thirteen years of age, would hold shovels at the furnace to screen the gatherers. They worked from six to six, one week days, one week nights alternately, with Sundays off if they were lucky. Shifts lasting as long as twenty-four or even thirty-six hours had been known when boys were in short supply. Bowen thought that a government grant towards schools would be a good idea and he would have been willing to make his contribution. He wanted to start a works school and was trying to think of some way to encourage attendance at a place of worship. Bowen didn't think there was anything unhealthy about glassmaking. The heat was harmless, there was not one unhealthy boy in the works and he felt the boys were kindly treated. Since there was only one run-down school in the area, the children were mostly rough and untaught in Nailsea and they appeared to be little cared for. They idled in crowds and were illiterate and ignorant. One of the boys interviewed had worked thirty-six hours at a stretch. He took his meals during the fifteen-minute breaks for refuelling kilns. He had been in gentleman's service before and on a farm, but he preferred the glassworks. He was a non-reader, but said he knew the letters. This was just three years before the Education Act of 1870 provided a legal framework for a basic education for all children.

In the early 1900s an account of the history of the works was written by Francis Mountain, who had been a blower there. Writing at the age of seventy-two, he says that in 1858 sheet-blowers came from Belgium and France. They lived in a row of cottages known as French Rank (recently demolished). They left in 1870, presumably to fight for their country when the Franco-Prussian War broke out. He mentions the names of a number of glass-blowers and other workers and particular blowers' names can be found on some of the labels on pieces in the Challicom Collection at Taunton Castle.

A letter from John M. Eyres dated 10 July 1911 to H. St George Gray, prompted by Eyres having read Gray's article on Nailsea Glass in *The Connoisseur*, contains much interesting information. He had worked as a youth in the packing rooms and office at Nailsea and he mentions having seen many times during the summer of 1862, many a red hot bulb whirled into a crown table before the flashing furnace and placed with infinite care into an annealing kiln and that he had never seen anywhere a more beautiful process than its manufacture. Wages were about £4 a week for a good blower and the unquenchable thirst of the blowers and gatherers was induced by hot working conditions. Snail-eating, apparently not just a continental custom, was also a local one in Somerset. The snails were heated at the furnace; it has been suggested that the juice from the snails was thought to prevent silicosis and therefore also indulged in by local miners. Eyres mentions an Irishman, James Kelly, a mixer of coloured glass who introduced the undulating/interlocking principle (see plate 55). A carafe of pale greenish tinge decorated with enamel looping from the Challicom Collection at Taunton is attributed to James Kelly (see plate 33). French blowers are mentioned by name and one of these, Desguin, is named as the maker of a pale green top hat in the Challicom Collection.

Eyres also wrote an autobiography. He names Tom Greaves, a glass-cutter who was also skilled at making all kinds of fancy glass. He made Eyres a splendid kaleidoscope. Charles Bryant was thought to be one of the best blowers. Eyres describes a brass band formed at the works, which, when a Volunteer Corps was later formed, became the band of the First Somersetshire Engineers. Nailsea was a lively place

5 The Nailsea Glassworks. This photograph, taken in the 1860s, shows men of the Royal Engineers Company (Volunteers), recruited from the staff of the glassworks.

in the sixties and there was a growing demand for labour. The brass band helped to keep the men together. There were weekly entertainments and concerts occasionally. Of the already twice-bankrupt Samuel Bowen he says,

> . . . travelling by night, selling his goods and settling his accounts by day, doing his office work on Saturday night, Sunday morning or whenever he could catch an opportunity; turning up at the Independent Chapel on Sunday evenings and leading the choir . . . he was renting a farm; but his knowledge of agriculture was faulty, I fear, as was his wisdom in coal mining. Even in that direction he tried his hand, sinking a lot of other people's money down a shaft and bringing up nothing in return but a lot of poor soft stuff of coal, scarcely worth burning.

Failure was once again to ensnare Samuel Bowen and in July 1869 operations ceased, about 300 men and boys, including the office staff, having to stop work.

> . . . Mr Bowen eventually paid his creditors two shillings and sixpence in the pound. Many of the more skilful workmen had been earning very good wages for several years, but taking them as a whole they were a very improvident lot and had saved but little; the consequence was, before many weeks were over, those who had not managed to secure situations elsewhere, skilful or unskilful, were 'on their beam ends' as a sailor would say. There was dire distress in Nailsea. To the credit of the neighbouring gentry, be it said, a relief fund was started to enable the workmen to tide over bad times in some measure, but, even so, it was a sorry spectacle to see men who had recently been earning from £2 to £4 a week, helping to make cinder paths by the roadside for a pittance of about two shillings a day.

Perhaps the glassmakers should have the last say. Here are the words of a traditional glassmakers' song:

> Bonny's backed the winner
> We're on the booze today
> We'll have a goose for dinner
> And drink whiskey in our tay
> We'll line our coats with five
>   pound notes
> And drink our noses blue
> For Bonny's backed the winner
> And we don't care what we do!

3 A CLASSIFICATION OF NAILSEA GLASS

When making a classification of Nailsea glass it must be remembered that the Nailsea firm was one of a number of window and bottle glass manufacturers both in the Bristol area and in many other parts of the country. Window glass and bottles were the mainstay of the glass industry. The typical product, the flask, the rolling-pin, the cream bowl, the walking-stick, the top hat and so on, so often associated with Nailsea itself, was also a product of other factories. Such articles were often catalogued by a company, such as those listed by Chance Brothers in 1868 (see page 9), sometimes made for the glass-blower himself from pot remains or bottoms, perhaps for use at home or as a purely decorative frigger, a demonstration of the skills and ingenuity of the individual glass-blower. Individual they certainly were and the variety of article produced and the variations on a single theme, for example walking-sticks, is astonishing. That Nailsea should have been given the credit for the style is their good fortune and a tribute to the Nailsea men. Perhaps they did produce more 'end of day' wares and friggers, possibly with more creative flair than in other centres, but it would be dangerous to state categorically that this was so. Nevertheless south-west England is very well endowed with fine public and private collections, particularly of the window and bottle glass items. Collections open to the public and worthy of mention are a very well-displayed and comprehensive collection at the National Trust property of Clevedon Court, Bristol City Art Gallery and Taunton Castle in the South West, and in London, the Victoria and Albert Museum. Many of the photographs in this book are of pieces in these collections.

H. St George Gray, curator of the Castle Museum, Taunton, from 1901 to 1949, was the author of three very informative articles on Nailsea glass. Reliable records and research, however, have revealed some puzzling omissions of types of glasses made there. The first of these articles in *The Connoisseur* deals with a fine collection of Nailsea glass that had been assiduously collected by Mrs Bertha Agnes Challicom, of Scarthingswell, Clevedon, and mostly acquired in and around Nailsea in the early years of this century. The renown of this collection and Mr Gray's article would appear to have given impetus to the popularity and collecting of Nailsea glass, and the article itself probably became the authoritative reference on the subject.

The second article dealt with another fine collection, this one formed by Mr John Lane, again obtained locally and in the South West. The third article mainly concerned itself with business and family records and statistics to do with the Nailsea firm. These included the abstracts of balance and accounts for the years 1807 to 1828 destroyed in Plymouth during the war, together with information recorded by others, including the letter from J. M. Eyres, a clerk at Nailsea between 1862 and 1869.

The Challicom article includes much detailed description of the pieces in the collection, a very good half of which was bequeathed to the Taunton Museum in 1939 (the other half went to the Bristol City Art Gallery), and a great deal of good background and historical references. What St George Gray overlooked, however, was that the Nailsea factory was a crown window (later sheet) glass factory, with bottle interests in the early years. Mrs Challicom's collection embraces many items, particularly flasks, made in glasses other than pale green window or bottle glasses. These flasks are of clear (flint) and coloured or white enamel glasses, which would not have been made at Nailsea. Although they were mostly collected in and around Nailsea they could well have been made in Bristol or elsewhere, for Nailsea families, particularly glassmaking families, could easily have acquired them. Glassworkers at Nailsea would have had contacts with their fellows in Bristol, some of them perhaps being inter-related. Bristol and Nailsea pieces could have been exchanged, and the movement of glassmakers to and from more distant glass-manufacturing regions would account for pieces being found far from their places of actual manufacture. The enamel used for decoration so often at Nailsea was easily obtainable in Bristol, where it was a speciality, in the form of rod or cullet.

H. St George Gray accepted that most of Mrs Challicom's pieces were authentic, with reservations, namely that investigations should be made on the site to discover what kind of glass fragments could be found there. But later writers, using St George Gray's article as the main reference source, perpetuated the idea that articles in metals other than window and bottle glasses were made at Nailsea, particularly if they were decorated with latticinio or with flecks or if they were articles like flasks or walking-sticks. The toys and friggers that began to be associated with Nailsea were, in fact, traditional products of glassmakers everywhere, including some travelling 'showmen' glassmakers who set up their mobile workshops in towns and country markets and fairs throughout the land.

In later years, in correspondence with Sir Hugh Chance, St George Gray agreed that not all the pieces in the Challicom Collection could have been made at Nailsea, but by then the myth was well established.

'Nailsea' had come to describe not necessarily the place of origin of a particular piece of glass, but a style practised by many glassworks.

CATEGORIES OF NAILSEA GLASS

1 Crown and sheet window glass of a pale green tinge. These were 'soda-lime' glasses and the standard 'sodium sulphate' (SS) mixture was composed of sixteen parts sand, six parts dry sodium sulphate, five parts of hydrate of lime, twelve parts of cullet and small amounts of charcoal, arsenic and manganese. There was also a 'carbonate' mixture of slightly different composition. (Coathupe's Works Notebook, 1836.)

Crown window glass panes were made in the following way: A blob of molten glass was gathered on to a blowpipe and blown into a large sphere. An iron rod, known as a 'pontil' or 'punty' (Coathupe's Works Notebook, 1836), was attached to the sphere, opposite the blowpipe, which was then cracked off and the cooling sphere reheated in a blowing or glory hole. The pontil was rapidly rotated, which caused the bull to open out into a slightly concave disc, known as a table, which would measure about 50in diameter. The table was then separated from the pontil and placed in an annealing kiln, where it cooled gradually. After cooling the table was cut into small panes. The point where the pontil was attached, the 'bullion' or 'bull', was regarded as a waste product. The table weighed about 9lb and when cut would produce 11sq ft of 'quarries' and a few smaller squares (plates 6, 7).

6 A 'crown' or 'table' of window glass showing how it was divided into the usual eleven pieces, each of approximately one square foot. The 'crown' itself would ideally measure about 50in diam. The bull was considered to be a waste product, but was used as a cheaper second, and in the course of time, right up to the present day, it has become fashionable to use in imitation 'period' window frames. The waste around the edge could be cut into smaller panes and anything left over could be recycled as cullet for a new batch (see also plate 7 and description).

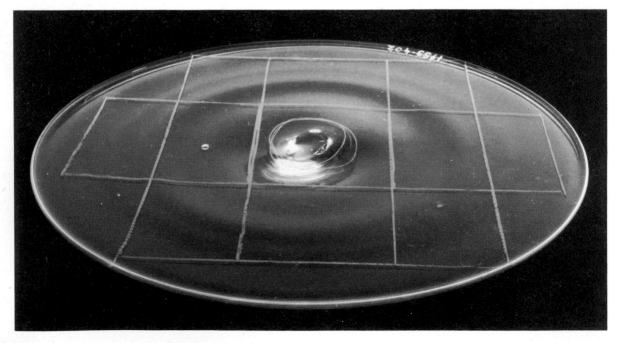

7 A pane of crown window glass, the basic product at Nailsea, showing the 'bullion', or 'bull', where the 'punty', or 'pontil rod', had been attached, in pale green metal, the characteristic 'Nailsea' colour. See also plate 6. See page 20, Categories of Nailsea Glass 1, for details of the ingredients used in making the glass and an account of the making of a 'crown table'.

2 Sheet glass was blown into a long cylinder in a flattening kiln and after reheating it was opened out to form a sheet of glass and then annealed.

3 Flashed sheet glass was standard sheet glass given a layer of colour. The coloured metal, ruby, blue or amber, was melted in a subsidiary furnace, known as a 'monkey' furnace. This coloured metal was very dense and would have transmitted very little light if blown directly into sheet glass. So the flashing process was used and this involved making a 'post' gathering of the coloured metal on the end of the blowpipe and then covering this with successive gatherings of clear sheet metal. As the bull was blown out into a cylinder the flashing metal expanded into a thin layer of colour on the inside, which did not absorb too much light.

One of the parisons shown in plate 50 seems to have been made on this principle, with the addition of white latticinio threads on the outside which would have been applied from a lump of white enamel glass, heated on a punty and then drawn out into a thread and wound round the parison and combed. There is a flask in the Challicom Collection at Taunton which could have been fashioned from such a parison and one wonders whether this type of flask could possibly have been made at the subsidiary furnace which was set up for the production of fancy glass and mentioned by Eyres in his letter to

H. St George Gray. Its date of manufacture would then be sometime in the 1860s.

Flashing metal could have been used for looped decoration in blue and red, on carafes for example (see plates 34, 61). It could also have been used solely to form a blown vessel and it is worth considering the origins of two very dense dark red, apparently black witch balls, illustrated in plate 96. There is also a bowl at Taunton, described as being made of black opaque glass, which has a certain redness when held up to the light. An excess of copper, incorporated in the glass batch to produce a ruby colour, or repeated reheating of the vessel, would have resulted in a progressive darkening of the coloured element.

Summary of Main Types of Nailsea Glass and Wares

1   Crown and sheet window glasses of a pale greenish tinge, a natural colour, which varies according to the amount of iron traces present in the sand used in the batch.

2   Dark bottle glass of various natural blackish-green shades. It varies from a distinctly greenish colour, soft and soapy in appearance and touch, to a brownish-golden green, particularly apparent when held to the light, the actual shade determined by the amount of iron oxide added to the recipe to darken the metal as required.

Domestic and other useful ware, flasks and friggers were made from these glasses, often decorated with loops and/or flecks of white and coloured enamel. Such wares were definitely made at Nailsea, Bristol and elsewhere in the eighteenth and nineteenth centuries.

3   Domestic wares, flasks and friggers in clear and coloured and white enamel glasses (some of Bristol manufacture), not actually of Nailsea origin, but made and decorated in what has come to be called the Nailsea style.

4   Set pieces, such as ships at sea, floral arrangements, birds and fountains and individual animals and miscellaneous items in all types of glasses, often made by the travelling 'showmen' glassmakers, from glass rods, heated by a blow lamp and drawn out into threads. It is difficult to say what items in this category were made at Nailsea, but such pieces are often referred to as Nailsea glass.

Pale green window glass and clear glass
It does seem unlikely from the evidence available that articles were made at Nailsea from clear glass, particularly flint glass. It is worth remembering, however, that the pale green tinge of window glass is sometimes hard to detect, particularly when thin blown, and there are

examples of vessels which appear to be made of clear, colourless metal, but which on very close examination reveal the pale green tinge, perhaps on the thicker part of a handle or in the base. A case in point is the Elton carafe, in which the pale green tinge is very difficult to detect except on the folded foot, which is decidedly green (see plate 61).

4 ANCESTRY AND INFLUENCES

Although it is interesting in itself to have a specialised knowledge of a particular type of glass it is also worthwhile considering it in the wider context of the whole history of the craft, and noting possible influences and affinities with other periods of glass manufacture.

The Victoria and Albert Museum has a fine representative selection of glass of all periods and cultures and a walk amongst the cabinets there enables appropriate and significant comparisons to be made. The pieces now referred to are in this collection unless otherwise stated.

Glass was possibly first made by the Ancient Egyptians, who began using it as a glaze c4000 BC. They made hollow vessels by threading molten glass round central cores of sand. These vessels were often decorated by applying threads of coloured glass and combing them; some vessels were splashed with flecks of contrasting colours. Similarities in form are sometimes evident between Egyptian amphoriskos and English early nineteenth-century scent bottles (cf plates 105 and 106). In the early Islamic period fine blown bottles, bowls and phials were made in light transparent green metal, sometimes with applied decoration. Other early periods worth examining are the Syrian, Roman and Teutonic. A clear greenish bottle from Syria has maroon swirls and there is a vase with purple striations moulded in low relief. White threaded decoration on a Roman brown glass bowl and spiralled threads round the body of a Teutonic bottle of greenish glass, fifth to seventh century AD, can be seen in plates 109 and 110.

Much of the Nailsea ware decorated in latticinio style is crude compared to the Venetian, but the influence was undoubtedly felt and there are some fine examples. Latticinio is derived from the Italian *latte*, meaning milk. The term is now used very generally to describe threaded decoration on glassware. It is a technique perfected by Venetian glassmakers in the sixteenth and seventeenth centuries and they produced much beautiful, intricate and sensitively executed work of this kind to decorate and embellish tazzas, plates, vases, wine glasses and other vessels. Threads can be applied to a parison by insertion in a mould lined with enamel canes or by having molten threads wound round the parison by hand (see plate 50). When applied it is marvered in by rolling the parison on a slab (marver) to embed the threads in it. The parison can be blown into a required hollow shape, the threads expanding into the final pattern as the vessel takes shape. The technique is also employed to make the twist or filigree stems of wine glasses, when the parison would be drawn out to some length and then cut into sections to provide the stems. And of course, some of those typical friggers attributed to Nailsea, walking-sticks, could have been made in this way.

Spanish and French glass of the seventeenth and eighteenth centuries was often heavily splashed and mottled with white and coloured enamel (see plates 114 and 115). A ship glass surmounted by a bugle, Dutch seventeenth century, is an aristocratic forerunner of the wrought and spun glass ships often attributed to Nailsea and Bristol (see plates 86 and 116).

In England the bottle glass factories were producing wares other than bottles long before the Nailsea enterprise was established. Such examples are a large tankard of dark green glass with horizontally applied threads with three seals inscribed B. Warren and dated 1700, and a bulbous jug with handle and foot, sealed Philip Sergeant 1717 (see plate 117). There is also a wine glass of clear flint metal with drawn stem and trumpet bowl, the whole decorated with continuous opaque white enamel spirals. And possibly from Bristol, and contemporary with Nailsea, there is a jug of opaque white enamel glass embedded with fragments of green, blue and red, late eighteenth or early nineteenth century (see plate 103). In Cheltenham Art Gallery and Museum is a pale green flagon with a seal dated 1777, pre-dating the founding of the Nailsea firm by eleven years.

History of Window Glass Manufacture

Crown glass glazing was carried out at an early date in the Near East and later practised by the Romans. There was a small production in England under the Roman occupation (see plates 107–8). In the seventh century AD glaziers came from Gaul to work at Jarrow and Wearmouth, according to Bede, at the request of the Abbot of Wearmouth. Making window glass by the crown method was probably introduced into Britain on a more substantial scale at the time of the Norman Conquest. Normandy had a tradition of specialist glassmaking families. By the thirteenth century window glass manufacture was taking place in the Weald. Cylinder and broad sheet glass manufacture was possibly introduced into Britain by glassmakers from Lorraine, who came to Britain to work for Carré in the sixteenth century. More well known for his 'façon de Venise' establishment in London, he monopolised window glass manufacture in the Weald. Round about this time the glass industry was being established in Bristol.

There is an interesting parallel to the Nailsea story in America. Mention has already been made of the regular consignments, from the Nailsea firm and others in the Bristol area, of window glass and bottles to New York and Philadelphia from the port of Bristol and recorded in detail in the Bristol Presentments.

Perhaps Nailsea flasks and other items also found their way across the Atlantic, possibly acquired as personal possessions by ships' crews. In 1907, John Gaynor, of the Salem glassworks, New Jersey, who had worked at Nailsea from 1831 to 1866, wrote to the Bristol Museum giving details of Nailsea's activities. Perhaps he is one example of a movement of glassmakers to and fro across the Atlantic from time to time, carrying with them stylistic influences. There are Nailsea flasks in the Metropolitan Museum of Art, New York.

Although a growing country could not supply all its own glass requirements, America had its own industry. It was a vital industry, becoming ever more important, and producing a fine range of wares, in addition to the basic production of window glass and bottles, with a striking individuality of their own.

Between 1739 and 1781 the Wistar factory produced window glass, pharmaceutical glass and bottles, and as other glasshouses sprang up in South Jersey to meet the increasing demand for these products, many objects were made in what has become known as the South Jersey tradition. In South Jersey factories many wares were free-blown in window and bottle glass in various shades of green and amber, and sometimes in aquamarine, pale blue or amethyst, such as jugs, milk pans and pitchers.

Very popular was lily-pad ware, made by dipping a jug or pitcher and forming a second layer of glass which was then tooled by hand and cut away to form the required shape.

American glasshouses created their own flask tradition with moulded designs depicting American history and customs. Between 1787 and 1830 the Pitkin works in New England made attractive flasks, which were swirled and ribbed in a variety of ways by moulding in relief.

By about 1840, loops and swirls of the latticinio kind were applied to vessels and much of this type of glass was made towards the end of the nineteenth century, in the South Jersey glasshouses. The similarity to Nailsea vessels is often striking.

5 THE WARE

8   A display of pale green window glass items at Clevedon Court. The pale green is not of one uniform tint, but varies from a pale emerald green to a yellowish green to a bluish green, and the actual intensity of the colour depends on the thickness of the metal and varies even in a single piece. *Top shelf*: a variety of hats; *middle shelf*: a pair of stoppered decanters, a pair of medicine bottles with 'tot' stoppers, a jug, a rolling-pin, a pane of crown window glass; *lower shelf*: an ear trumpet, a cucumber trainer, a pair of flagons, a pair of knitting needles, a large globe or witch ball and two lumps of glass, one with intrusions of white enamel.

Examples of the above items are dealt with individually elsewhere, except for the large globe or witch ball, which has been decorated in the style of Decalcomania or Potichomania, described in 1855 by Charles Dickens as 'a pretty ladylike employment of considerable variety and application'. The art entailed embellishing the inside surface of the globe with cut-outs, which had to be carefully glued. A coat of varnish sealed the cut-outs to the whole interior surface and a chalk or plaster lining or paint was applied as an opaque background to give a unity to the separate cut-out elements of the design. It has been suggested that the effect obtained was in imitation of decorated porcelain.

9 Jug of pale green metal with threaded rim of the same metal and roughly engraved H. Woodman (*height 5½in Clevedon Court*).

A label on the base dates this piece c1835, although there appears to be a date partially and roughly engraved in outline 17..7. Such pieces are usually described as late eighteenth or early nineteenth century, so either date above would be reasonable. This style of jug is quite common, in various sizes and is found in dark bottle metal as well (see plate 38). There is a larger jug of this type in the same collection, and of a very attractive pale blue.

10   A fine pair of rare plain decanters with squared stoppers in pale green metal (*height 9in   Clevedon Court*).

A label on the underside of one of the decanters is marked c1780. The form of the decanters is like the so-called Bristol green and blue decanters often applied with gilt labels indicating the contents, like Gin, Rum, or Shrub. The stoppers are unusual (the Bristol ones are often pear-shaped and flat) and are the same as the type of stopper often found on pharmaceutical jars or bottles of the same period. The metal has interesting irregularities, bubbles and striations which add to their charm and which are typical of the period in this type of glass. If the date of 1780 is accurate then they are pre-Nailsea pieces and were likely to have been made in one of the Bristol crown houses.

11   *Left*: hat of pale greenish-brown metal, probably bottle glass with spiral threads of white enamel of varying thickness round the inside of the rim (*height 2in*); *right*: hat of pale green metal (*height 2in   Clevedon Court*).

Hats were a typical 'frigger' product of the glass-blowers. They vary in size from the very small variety illustrated here to those almost big enough to wear. They may have been made as a test of an apprentice's skill to demonstrate the degree of mastery he had acquired of the craft he was learning, and besides having a purely decorative function it has been suggested that they were used at table as toothpick holders, salt containers or, if big enough, to contain celery.

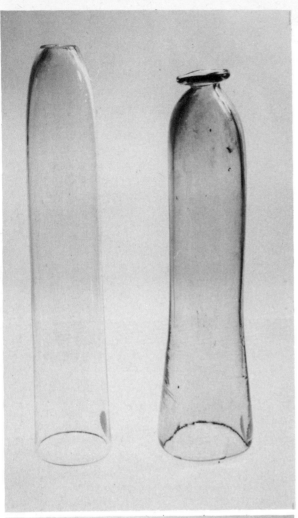

12 *Left*: a cucumber trainer or straightener in pale green metal (*height 14½in*). Very similar in form to the adjacent ear trumpet, but without the everted rim which forms the ear piece and of thinner metal. The cucumber flower would have been inserted in the narrower end of this very practical piece. A simple and most effective horticultural aid; *right*: an ear trumpet in pale green metal, narrowing towards the top and with a pronounced everted rim as an ear piece (*height 13½in, diam 3in Clevedon Court*). The author and a friend who possesses a similar one carried out tests and can guarantee its efficiency! An elderly and fragile person, however, might have found it too heavy to hold for any length of time without support.

13 An inkwell in pale green metal (*diam about 3 to 4in Clevedon Court*).

One of a number of shapes that were produced in both window and bottle glasses.

14 A pair of moulded flat-sided medicine bottles in pale green metal with 1¾in tot stoppers (H. Pochet's patent) (*height 7in   Clevedon Court*).

The clear glass tot stoppers are medicine glasses, each with a glass ferrule rising vertically from the centre and surrounded by a cork which fits into the bottle neck.

15 A flagon in pale green metal with a thick broad handle nicely pressed into the shoulder and a slight kick in the base (*height 11in   Clevedon Court*).

A common form found in a variety of sizes. There is a similar flagon at Clevedon, splashed in white enamel.

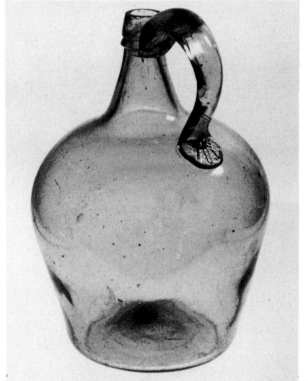

16   A decanter with stopper, gimmel flask and stopper and a carafe, all in apparently clear colourless metal and decorated with blotches of red and blue.

Gimmel flask or double flask possibly used to contain oil and vinegar (*height 7½in*); decanter with cork, brass mounted and engraved 'Rum' (*height 8in   Clevedon Court*).

Although these vessels appear to be of a clear colourless metal, similar vessels are to be found which do have the pale green tinge (cf plates 33 and 34).

17 *Left*: mug in dark blackish-green metal with large chips of white enamel marvered in (*height approx 5in*); *right*: handled bottle or jug in the same metal with streaks of enamel marvered in and crudely writhened (*height 6¾in Clevedon Court*).

The metal of these vessels has a distinct soft, soapy appearance and feel, something like serpentine.

18 A bowl in brownish golden-green metal, well covered in white enamel flecks, with an irregularly folded and everted rim (*diam 6½in Clevedon Court*).

19 A jug in brownish golden-green metal with white enamel flecks on body and threads round rim (*height 4¼in Clevedon Court*).

20 *Left*: a round miniature flask with flat sides in dark reddish-brown metal with broadly applied white-enamel combed loops and swirls (*height approx 4in*); *right*: a round bottle or flask in golden-green metal; a very flat-sided and narrow vessel (*height 5in Clevedon Court*).

21 A cloche in brownish golden-green metal, intensely bubbled, waisted towards the base with a solid knob on the top (cf cloche, plate 68, in pale green window metal) (*height 9in, diam 8in Clevedon Court*).

22 Onion-shaped bottle in dark brownish-green metal, flecked with white enamel (*height 8½in Clevedon Court*).

23 Globular bottle in dark brownish-green metal flecked with white enamel (*height 8½in Clevedon Court*).

There is a bottle of similar form to 23, and attributed to Nailsea, at Taunton Castle Museum. Perhaps bottles 22 and 23 are the types of bottle manufactured at Stanton Wick up to 1815 and at Nailsea in the early years. Sir Hugh Chance mentions a fairly recent visit to Stanton Wick, where he found fragments of blackish bottles of bulbous form with high kick-ups.

24 Jar or vase of dark green metal flecked with white enamel, some of the flecks having pale pink centres (*Clevedon Court*).

25 Jug in dark green metal with streaks of enamel marvered and writhened in. Another soft, soapy piece (*height approx 6in Clevedon Court*).

26 Aiguière or water bottle in reddish-brown metal, decorated with combed loops of white enamel (*height 5¼in Clevedon Court*).

A similar metal to that of the flask illustrated in plate 20. Possibly a Bristol piece (cf Spanish water bottle, plate 113).

27 *Facing page, left*: 'Bristol' blue footed bowl decorated with wavy loops of white enamel (*height 2¾in, diam 5in*); *right :* jug of the same metal and decoration (*height 4in   Clevedon Court*).

Both late eighteenth or early nineteenth century. This blue metal has a decidely amethyst tinge and these items could very well have been made in one of the Bristol flint houses.

28 'Bristol' blue jug with white enamel latticinio decoration (*height 4¾in*); a matching bowl, of same height, with cover (*Clevedon Court*).

29 General display of dark bottle glass items and pipes, mostly in coloured flint and opaque white glass (*Clevedon Court*). On the centre shelf of the case there are a few animals – swans and pigs – and a loom. Such articles were sometimes made by travelling glassmakers who set up shop at country fairs and markets. More ambitious pieces were also produced and there is a fine collection of wrought and spun ships and set pieces of fountains with birds and flowers.

30 A bottle in pale green metal flecked with white, pale amber and blue (*height 5·7in, diam of base 2·5in Challicom Collection 1939, ref no 2263, Taunton Castle*).

31 A bottle in pale green metal, with a rough writhen surface, and streaked with white and amber. Pronounced kick in base (*height 6·5in, diam of base 3·2in   Challicom, ref no 2264, Taunton*).

32 A bottle in pale green metal of smooth surface and streaked in blue and white (*height 8·6in, diam of base 2·5in Challicom, ref 2262, Taunton*).

33 A carafe with latticinio decoration in opaque white (*neck 3·8in, body 4in × 6·7in Challicom, ref 2282, Taunton*). Made by James Kelly. J. M. Eyres mentions a craftsman of this name in his letter to H. St George Gray, so the date of manufacture would be in the 1860s.

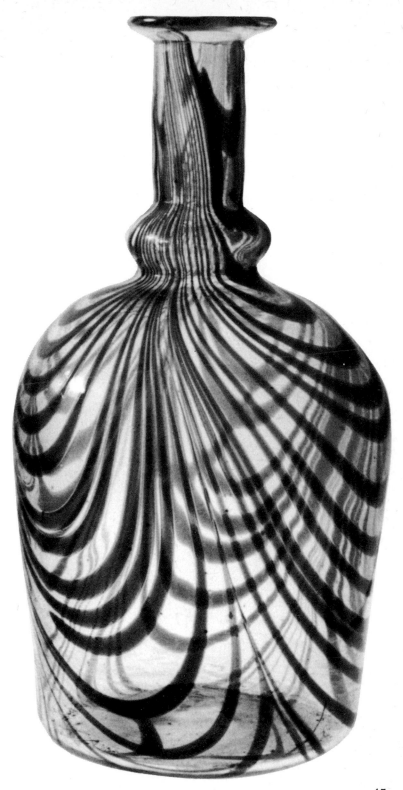

34 One of a pair of carafes of apparently clear glass, probably sheet metal, one with red and blue splashes and the other with blue latticinio (*height 11½in and 11in Challicom, ref 2287 and 2286, Taunton*) (see also frontispiece).

45

35   A shade of pale green metal, used for hastening the ripening of grapes out of doors (*height 10½in donated by P. T. Marshall, 1939, ref 2261, Taunton*). Made in the nineteenth century in the form of a bell jar flattened on one side with an orifice on the shoulder of this flat side to fit over the bunch of grapes.

36   Bottle of dark green metal, of flat form, with large white flecks marvered in (*height 6·7in   donated by H. M. Gibbs, 1916, ref 2247, Taunton*).

37   A fireside ornament in pale green metal in the form of a hunted fox
(*height 4·8in, length 5·4in   Challicom, ref 2490, Taunton*).
    In the Hull Collection there is a cast metal ornament, almost identical, but
in reverse.

38–9 Two jugs in dark golden-green metal, showing two of the variations in style in which such vessels were made (*Taunton*).

40 Flask of dark golden-green metal, of flat form, with a few white enamel flecks (*height 6·8in Challicom, ref 2248, Taunton*).

41 Flask of dark golden-green metal, of flat form, with slight indentations for finger and thumb, with mostly white flecks, but one or two of red (*Challicom, ref 2276, Taunton*).

A similar flask in the collection has a label which reads, 'Old Nailsea Glass, bought at Nailsea in 1907 from the descendants of the maker'.

42 Three vases of dark green, blue-green and amber metal, each with a diam of about 3in (*Challicom, ref 2268, 2271, 2270, Taunton*).

The one of dark green glass has a label which reads, 'Old Nailsea Glass, bought at Weare, 1907, from an old lady of eighty years of age, who had it direct from the Nailsea Glassworks'. Vases of similar form were made by the Romans in pale green glass.

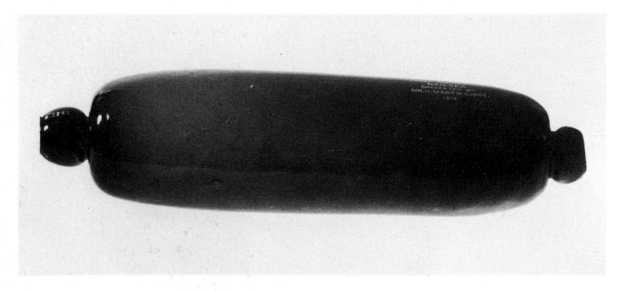

43 A rolling-pin or ship's bottle of dark greenish, golden brown metal with one knob open (*length 12½in*).

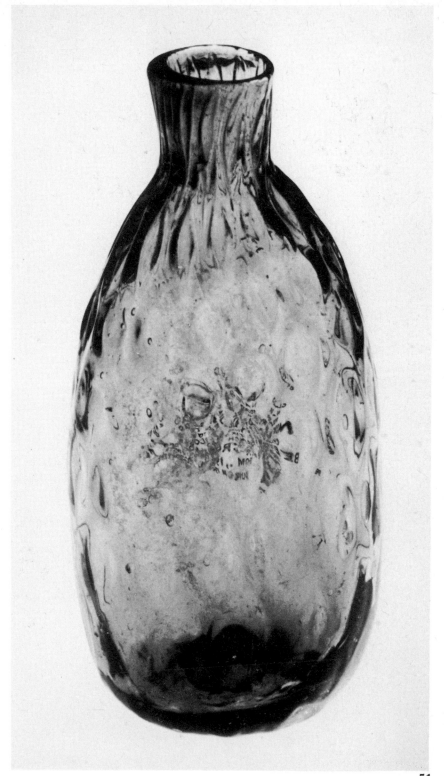

44 A flask or phial, of green metal, the surface 'nipped diamond ways' (*length approx 5in purchased 1941, ref 2045, Taunton*).

This flask was found embedded in mortar on top of the church tower at Beer Crocombe in 1936. It is probably of much earlier origin than Nailsea and the green metal, although pale, is darker than the Nailsea green. The 'nipped diamond ways' surface suggests a sixteenth- or seventeenth-century origin, but there is a witch ball in the Challicom Collection of a bluish green which has a surface fashioned in this way, and it is attributed to Richard Knight, 1790.

45 Flask in dark, but clear, green metal with combed latticinio decoration in white enamel. Pronounced indentation on the sides (*height 7·1in Challicom, ref 2280, Taunton*).

46 *Left*: flask in dark clear green metal with flecked decoration in opaque white, fairly pointed at the base (*height 6·3in   Challicom, ref 2275, Taunton*). This is a similar flask to 2274 (not illustrated), which has a label which reads, 'Old Nailsea Glass', bought in 1907 at Nailsea from the descendants of the maker; *right*: flask in dark clear green metal decorated with a broad white opaque white spiral running from end to end (*height 5·3in   Challicom, ref 2277, Taunton*).

47 *Left*: flask of translucent ruby tinted glass with spiral loops of opaque white encased in clear glass (*height 6·7in*); *right*: flask of clear glass decorated with combed loops of opaque white, red and blue (*height 8in   Challicom, ref 2410 and 2319, Taunton*).

48 Flask of pale distinctly yellowish-green metal with spiral decoration in translucent ruby bordered on either side by thin threads of opaque white (*height 5·9in Challicom, ref 2334, Taunton*).

49 Mug of apparently clear colourless glass, but a pale green tinge is faintly discernible (*height 3·8in Challicom, ref 2284, Taunton*).

A label reads, 'Old Nailsea Glass, made by Barnett'. Francis Mountain's account of the Nailsea glassworks lists I. Barnett as a crown blower. Both the metal and the looped decoration are similar to the Elton carafe and beaker (see plate 61). This is another example of metal which can easily be assumed to be of colourless metal, but which on examination reveals the greenish tinge where the glass is thicker.

50 Two parisons. *Left*: dark greenish-black bottle glass with white enamel flecks (*diam 1·6in*); *right*: ruby glass cased with clear glass decorated with combed latticinio in opaque white (*diam 1·7in Challicom, ref 2511 and 2514, Taunton*).

The parison is the globule of glass prepared for blowing. A gathering is made from molten metal and any decoration, for example, the flecks or threads of white enamel, are then applied to the surface and marvered in on a flat metal slab called a marver. The example on the right is particularly intriguing. A gathering was first made by gathering up a blob of dense ruby metal, which was then encased in a layer or layers of clear glass and finally decorated with white threads and then combed. The first two parts of this process are identical to the procedure for preparing a parison for blowing a cylinder for flashed sheet glass, which was advertised by the firm in the 1860s (see page 21, 'Categories of Nailsea Glass').

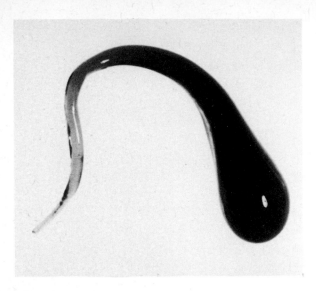

51–3 Prince Rupert's Drop. A tadpole-shaped piece of glass in a greenish, yellow-brown metal (*length approx 2in   Challicom, ref 2481, Taunton*).

This is one of two drops in the Challicom Collection, the other being of pale green metal. To Christopher Merrett's translation of 1662 of *Ars Vitraria,* by Antonio Neri, an early authoritative treatise on glass manufacture, is appended *An Account of the Glass Drops,* made by the Royal Society meeting at Gresham College, and the reader is referred to pages 354–5 of *The Art of Glass,* photographed in plate 53.

Prince Rupert, military and naval commander, and a man of wide interests and accomplishments, shared with his cousin, King Charles II, a keen interest in scientific investigations. They were both members of the Royal Society, where the glass drop experiment took place on 6 March 1661.

The Prince set up a laboratory at Windsor Castle, where he is reported to have 'dabbled in scientific experiments'. He discovered that drops of toughened glass could be made by dropping molten glass into cold water, a form of toughening illustrating the principle on which the development of toughened glass in the 20th century has been based. A drop withstands a heavy blow on the head but disintegrates into finely powdered glass if the tail is broken. It is an appropriate coincidence that Prince Rupert was particularly interested in ballistics and armaments, considering the explosive aspect of the glass drop experiment.

Samuel Pepys recorded in his diary on 13 January 1662 that after dinner a guest 'did show us the experiment . . . of the chymicall glasses which break all to dust by breaking off the little small end – which is a great mystery to me.'

The manufacture of the drops seems as if it might have been *the glasshouse practical joke.* They are mentioned by J. M. Eyres in his letter to H. St George Gray in which he says,

> . . . you do not describe those two little worm-like objects . . . but in my day, if you wanted to be initiated into the mysteries of glassmaking, either of the gatherers would be ready to oblige you. He would just gather a few ounces of melted glass at the end of a punty stick and drop a portion of it into a kettle of water. When cold enough he would fish it up with his fingers and offer you the thick end of it, bidding you to hold tight! As soon as he found you had a grasp of it, he would give the thin end a twist, when, hey, presto! you would find yourself with a handful of glass dust after a loud explosion, with a tingling sensation in your fingers and thumb which would last you for some time.

THE
Art of Glass,

WHEREIN

Are shown the wayes to make and colour Glass, Pastes, Enamels, Lakes, and other Curiosities.

Written in *Italian* by *Antonio Neri*, and Translated into *English*, with some Observations on the Author.

Whereunto is added an account of the Glass Drops, made by the Royal Society, meeting at *Gresham College.*

LONDON,

Printed by *A.W.* for *Octavian Pulleyn*, at the Sign of the *Rose* in St. *Pauls* Church-yard. MDCLXII.

Sir Hugh Chance provides this technical information:

> The Rupert's Drops were made by dropping a blob of glass from a gathering iron into cold water. This set up serious stresses as between the surface and interior, which when released by breaking the tail of the drop, caused it to explode.

Reference is made to them in an article, 'Friggers Afloat', by T. Taylor Seago in *The Lady*. The author says that they were popular with bargemen's children in the nineteenth century. With other friggers they would have been exchanged with novelties and goods obtained by the much travelled barge families who carried supplies of sand and coal to the glasshouses of northern England. The trick was experienced by the bargemen's children and probably also by the children of the glassblowers, who sometimes took their fathers' lunches and suppers along to the works (*The Lady,* 10 December 1959).

354   *An account of the Glaſs Drops.*
experiments to be made in any kinde whatſoever, as being done with exceeding exactneſs.

This account was given to the Society by Sir Robert Moray. MDCLXI.

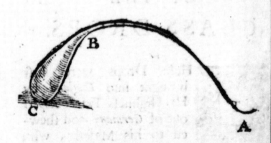

A B the thread, B C the body, B the neck, A the point or end of the thread.

They are made of *Green-glaſs* well refined; till the Metall (as they call it) be well refined, they do not at all ſucceed, but crack and break, ſoon after they are drop't into the water.

The

An account of the Glaſs Drops.   355
The beſt way of making them, is to take up ſome of the Metall out of the pot upon the end of an Iron rod, and immediately let it drop into cold water, and there lye till it cool.

If the Metall be too hot when it drops into the water, the Glaſs drop certainly roſts and cracks all over, and falls to pieces in the water.

Every one that Cracks not in the water, and lies in it, till it be quite cold, is ſure to be good.

The moſt expert Workmen, know not the juſt temper of heat, that is requiſite, and therefore cannot promiſe before hand to make one that ſhall prove good, and many of them miſcarry in the making, ſometimes two or three or more for one that hits.

Some of them froſt, but the body falls not into pieces; others break into pieces before the red heat be quite over, and with a ſmall noiſe; other ſoon after the red heat is over, and with a great noiſe; ſome neither break nor crack, till they ſeem to be quite cold; others keep whole whileſt they are in the water, and fly to pieces of themſelves with a ſmart noiſe as

Aa 2   ſoon

54 A coil of yellow spun glass and a table mat of woven spun glass in a
concentric pattern of blue and white (*diam 7in   Challicom, ref 2500, Taunton*).

There is a similar coil of glass, ref 2503, which apparently belonged to
Isaac White, one of the later managers of the Nailsea works. John M. Eyres
in his letter to H. St George Gray remembers seeing specimens of plaited
glass at the Nailsea works, but he never saw any made.

55 Sheet glass in pale green metal, finely ribbed and of the interlocking/undulating type, mentioned by J. M. Eyres in his letter to H. St George Gray. Identical except for colour to the piece of blue glass referred to on page 13 (*8in × 8in   G 3543, Bristol City Art Gallery*).

56 Two bottles in dark green glass, one sealed IBB, with white enamel
decoration (*height 6½in   G 696 and G 703, Bristol City Art Gallery*).

57 Bottle in dark green glass, with white enamel flecks and seal, JME 1833 (*height 10½in   N 8307, purchased by the friends of Bristol City Art Gallery, 1973*).

58 Mug in dark green glass, with white enamel flecks (*height 6in   G 691, Bristol City Art Gallery*).

59 Mug in dark green glass, with white enamel flecks. Of crude shape, perhaps an early apprentice's piece (*height 5½in   G 744, Bristol City Art Gallery*).

60 Bottle in dark green glass, flecked with white enamel, blown into octagonally shaped mould (*height 6in   G 698, Bristol City Art Gallery*).

61   Globular bottle or carafe of a very pale green metal, hardly discernible in the body of the vessel, but much more pronounced in the foot (*Clevedon Court*). The bottle has ruby looped decoration, but the folded foot is plain (having been formed separately). There is possibly a matching cup or beaker which in effect looks colourless. Both pieces are good examples of a green tinge so faint it is hardly detectable.

Attached to the bottle is an old and faded label which reads, '1799. Given to George Masters by Mr Stonier, Manager of Chance's Nailsea Works. Chance brought it to the June competition. George Masters presented it to Sir Edmund Elton in 1914.' If 1799 is recorded as a date of manufacture it is probably inaccurate. Mr W. Stonier was manager of the works from 1870, when Chance Brothers had taken over. George Masters was in the employment of Sir Edmund Elton and worked in his pottery. Another point is that the ruby looping has been proved by analysis to have a lead base, and is copper ruby, which was not introduced into Britain until Bontemps came to work for Chance Brothers in about 1850.

Carafes of this style were made in the latter half of the nineteenth century, and if this one was made at Nailsea, the ruby metal used for decoration could have been the same as that used for flashing sheet glass (which was manufactured at Nailsea in the sixties).

This carafe and beaker is in the possession of Lady Elton.

62 *Facing page*: two flasks, a jug and a rolling-pin in dark bottle glass, flecked or looped with opaque white enamel, typical of Bristol bottle manufacture at the end of the eighteenth or early nineteenth century (*collection, Sir Hugh Chance*).

63 A jug and flask in crown window glass metal, the jug with white enamel rim. Probably late eighteenth or early nineteenth century.
   In the foreground are two drumsticks, in pale green window glass, one with ruby centre (*collection, Sir Hugh Chance*).

64 *Below*: two carafes, the one on the left with ruby loops, the other with blue loops (*collection, Sir Hugh Chance*).
   These are typical of carafes made in window glass factories in the latter half of the nineteenth century.

65 *Left*: rolling-pin in clear window glass with blue loops; *centre*: two flasks, the top flask in opal metal with ruby and blue loops, the lower flask in white enamel with dark blue loops, probably Bristol, end of the eighteenth or early nineteenth century; *right*: rolling-pin flecked with ruby and blue. The insides of both coated with white plaster. Second half of the nineteenth century (*collection, Sir Hugh Chance*).

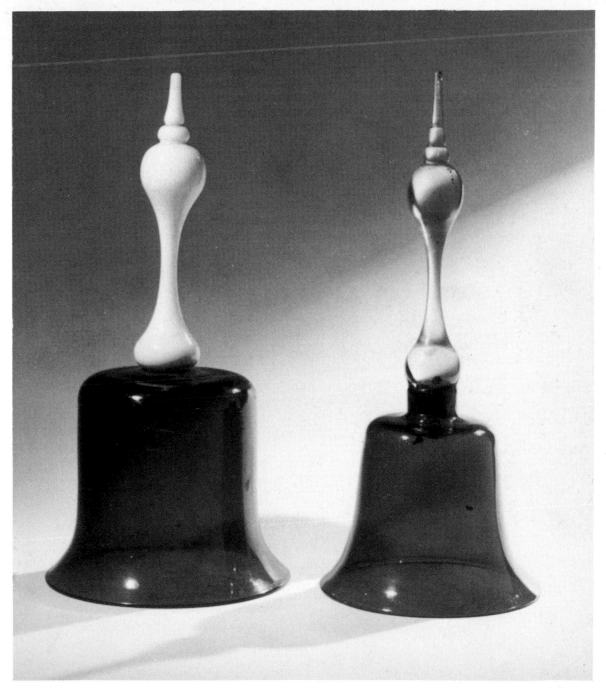

66 Two bells. *Left*: one of copper-green body and opal handle; *right*: bell with dark blue body and clear flint handle (*collection, Sir Hugh Chance*).

Bells are often attributed to Nailsea, but it is far more likely that they were made in Bristol and elsewhere and these two examples could come from a Bristol factory. End of the eighteenth or early nineteenth century.

67 Jug in pale green metal with white enamel rim kick in base, rough pontil. Probably late eighteenth or early nineteenth century (*height 8in   collection of Mr and Mrs S. J. Painter*).

68 Mid-nineteenth-century cloche in pale green metal (cf plate 21) (*height 7½in, diam 6in   collection of Mr and Mrs S. J. Painter*).

69   *Right*: wall oil lamp in pale green metal (*height 7½in, width 5½in   collection of Mr and Mrs S. J. Painter*).

70   *Below right*: A pestle, and a drumstick in pale green metal with a ruby and blue twist (*length approx 7in and 8in collection of Mr and Mrs S. J. Painter*).

71   *Below*: knitting needles in pale green metal (*length approx 12in collection of Mr and Mrs S. J. Painter*).

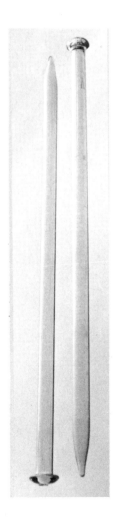

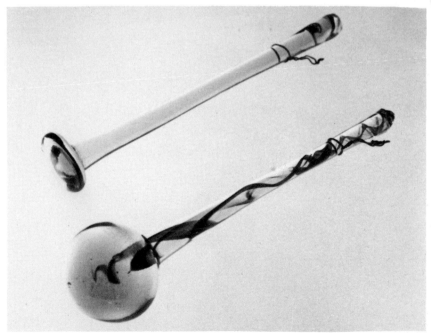

72   Three rolling-pins in pale green metal (*collection of Mr and Mrs S. J. Painter*). *Left*: flecked with red and blue, with plaster lining (*length 14½in*); *centre*: applied cut-out and plaster lining (*length 13in*); *right*: with combed blue loops (*length 13in*).

All these pins have both ends closed, but others were made with a stopper at one end. Salt or tea might have been stored inside the pin. Although some could have been used for rolling pastry, many were purely decorative and even given as love tokens, with affectionate messages inscribed on them.

70

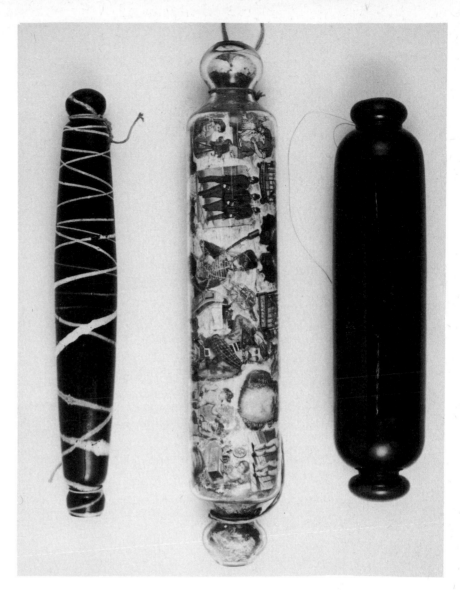

73 Three rolling pins (*collection of Mr and Mrs S. J. Painter*). *Left*: in dark bottle metal, with applied enamel threads (*length 11½in*); *centre*: in pale green metal with applied cut-outs and plaster lining in the style of Decalcomania or Potichomania (see page 28 and plate 8); *right*: in 'Bristol' blue metal (*length 17in*).

74 Preserve jar in the form of a barrel in dark golden brownish-green metal; cover missing (*height 4¼in   collection of Mr and Mrs S. J. Painter*).

75 Base of vessel showing rough pontil mark where the pontil rod was removed (*collection of Mr and Mrs S. J. Painter*).

As the nineteenth century progressed, the pontil was usually ground smooth, as clearly seen in the illustrations of the dairy bowl, plates 93 and 94, and the kick-ups shallower. These points may help in determining the age of an object.

76 A selection of walking-sticks (*collection of Mr and Mrs S. J. Painter*). *Left to right*: stick of pale green metal, the surface twisted 'barley-sugar' fashion, narrowing towards the end (*length 28½in*); stick of very pale green metal, with a finely writhened surface, broadening towards the end, a similar surface texture to Sir Hugh Chance's drumstick (see plate 63) (*length 34¼in*); stick in the form of a crook in ruby metal, the surface smooth and broadening towards the end, before finally tapering to point (*length 36in*); stick in 'Bristol' blue, tapering to a fine point (*length 39in*); stick in the form of a crook in ruby metal, unpolished, with an almost frosted appearance, and with a flat end (*length 34in*); stick in the form of a crook, in dark bottle metal, the surface twisted 'barley-sugar' fashion (*length 30in*).

The walking-stick or glass rod was a typical 'frigger' product of the glassmaker. Tradition has it that walking-sticks were hung in prominent places in the parlour. Believed to attract germs, they were wiped every morning. Decorative pieces made in endless variety, they exhibit the diverse skills of the glassmaker.

George Soane refers to superstitions in Devonshire in *Curiosities of Literature* of 1847:

> . . . the most curious of their general superstitions is that of the glass rod, which they set up clean in their houses, and wipe clean every morning, under the idea that all diseases from malaria will gather about the rod innoxiously. It is twisted in the form of a walking stick, and is from four to eight feet long. They can seldom be persuaded to sell, and if it gets broken, they argue that misfortune will ere long befall someone in the cottage where it has been set up.

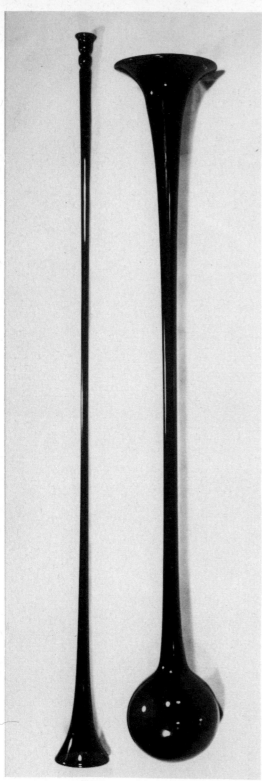

77 *Left*: a coach horn in blue metal, possibly Bristol (*length 41in, diam of mouthpiece 3in   collection of Mr and Mrs S. J. Painter*); *right*: a 'yard of ale' in ruby metal (*length 36in, diam of mouthpiece 5in   collection of Mr and Mrs S. J. Painter*).

78 *Facing page*: Gimmel flasks (*collection of Mr and Mrs S. J. Painter*). *Left*: flask in clear flint glass with random white enamel latticinio decoration with crimping on the sides and a blue rim; *right*: flask in clear flint glass with combed latticinio in opaque white.

Gimmel flasks are double flasks, and could have been used to hold oil and vinegar, for example.

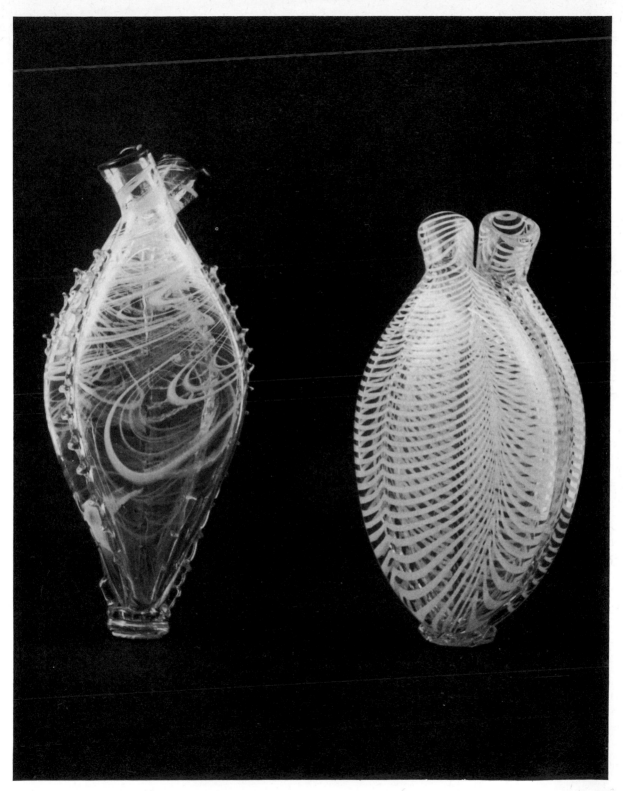

79 *Left*: flask in opaque white metal with combed pink latticinio decoration; *right*: flask in the same metal with pink and dark blue loops. The combination of these latter colours is often attributed to the Stourbridge district (see group of rolling-pin, pipe and flask, plate 84) (*collection of Mr and Mrs S. J. Painter*).

80 *Left*: flask of clear glass with combed loops in pink, surrounded by white enamel bands; *right*: flask in clear glass with combed pink loops and red rim (*collection of Mr and Mrs S. J. Painter*).

81 Flasks in the form of bellows (*collection of Mr and Mrs S. J. Painter*). *Left*: flask in clear glass with crimped edges and applied prunts; *right*: flask similar but with brownish-red and white loops.

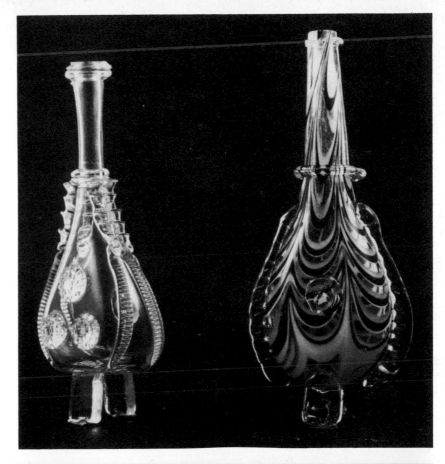

82 *Left*: flask in light apple-green metal with combed loops of a very pale green; *right*: flask covered entirely with loops of orange and yellow (*collection of Mr and Mrs S. J. Painter*).

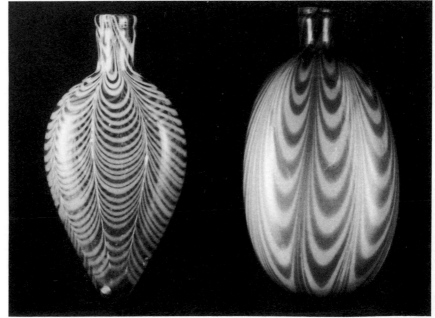

83 *Left*: flask in Bristol blue metal; *right*: flask in clear metal with white and reddish-brown combed loops (*collection of Mr and Mrs S. J. Painter*).

The flasks described above and illustrated in plates 78 to 83 measure between 6 and 8in. Small flasks were often used for containing liquid refreshment and were used by travellers.

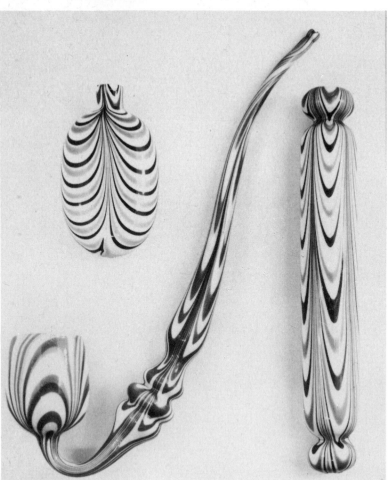

84 A 'Stourbridge trio' of flask, pipe and rolling-pin, in opaque white metal with pink and blue combed loops (see plate 79) (*collection of Mr and Mrs S. J. Painter*).

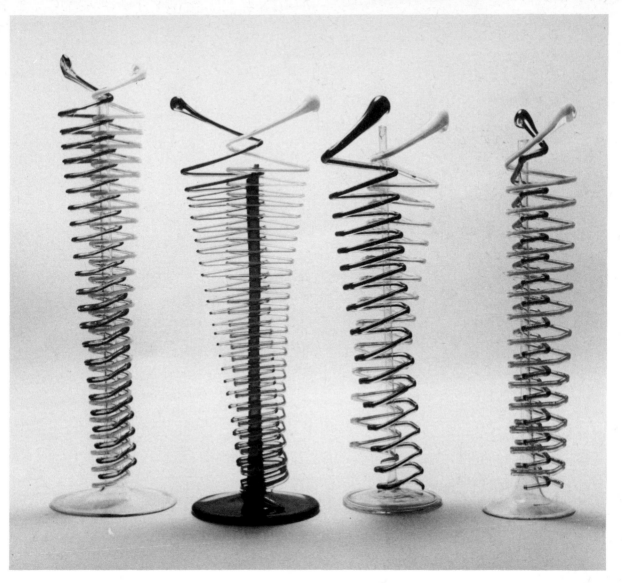

85   Jacob's Ladders (*collection of Mr and Mrs S. J. Painter*).
Each ladder consists of two interlocking angled spirals formed from coloured enamel rods encased in clear glass placed over a hollow drawn stem and circular folded foot. One of these 'stands' is in dark yellowish-green bottle metal. They are fine 'frigger' examples of the glassmaker's virtuosity.

86 *Facing page*: a ship in clear glass with pink hull, anchor, jack tars aloft and flags in red, white and blue enamel; small boat alongside in pale blue enamel, white enamel lighthouse set in a fibre glass sea. It has a protective glass dome (*height approx 12in   collection of Mr and Mrs S. J. Painter*).

Such pieces have often been attributed to Bristol and Nailsea. They were probably made in a number of glassmaking regions and sometimes trailed and spun by travelling glassmakers who set up their mobile workshops in towns, at country fairs and markets and made such pieces to order. Other set pieces were also popular and included fountains adorned with flowers and birds. Some good examples are at Clevedon Court, including a centre piece of King Solomon's Temple with the crowned monarch standing under a floral arch.

87 Deer and hounds in white enamel and a fox in the foreground in amber glass (*height about 1in   collection of Mr and Mrs S. J. Painter*).

88   Birds in white enamel, with coloured spun-glass tails on stands of clear glass (*height 6–9in   collection of Mr and Mrs S. J. Painter*).

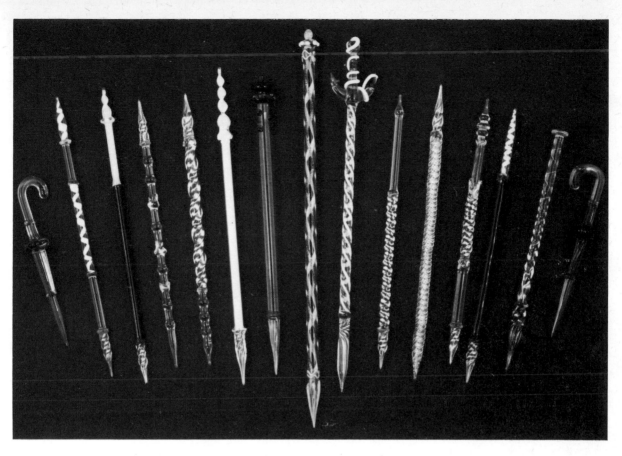

89 Toy pens, mostly in clear glass, decorated in white and coloured enamels and surface twists (*height 5–8in   collection of Mr and Mrs S. J. Painter*).

90 Two lacemakers' lamps, in pale green metal, not quite identical in colour, both with many small air bubbles (*height approx 5in; saucers 4in across collection of Mr John Williams*).

91 Hat in pale green metal (*height 3in, front to back 5¾in; between turned up rims 4in collection of Mr John Williams*).

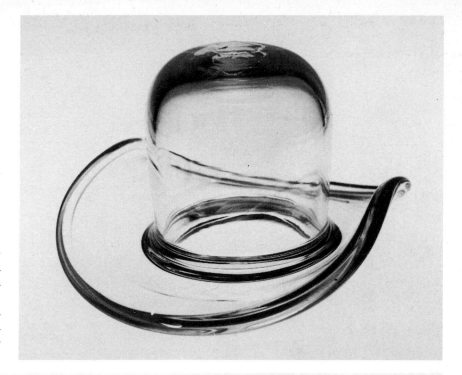

92 *Left*: flask in dark olive-green metal flecked with white enamel; *right*: jug in dark green metal, of soft, soapy type with writhened streaks of white enamel (*height 7in and 4½in collection of Mr John Williams*).

93   Dairy bowl for cream separation, in pale green metal. Folded rim and pouring lip, the rim being hollow (*diam, rim to rim, 19in, diam across base 12in, depth from rim to base varies from 3½ to 4½in   collection of Mr John Williams*).
    Rim and base very worn, showing that it was once constantly used.

94   *Facing page*: dairy bowl, illustrated and described in plate 93, seen from above (*collection of Mr John Williams*).
    Note the ground pontil.

95 *Above*: three rolling-pins in dark olive-green metal. *Top*: no decoration (*length 15¾in*); *centre*: roughly engraved, stipple fashion with the words *Arun, Susanna*, a sailing ship and a steam and sail ship, a bridge and the sun and simple geometric patterns (*length 15in*); *bottom*: flecked with mostly white, but some blue, red and yellow enamel (*length 13¾in   collection of Mr John Williams*).

96 *Facing page, below*: pair of witch balls in deep ruby metal (of black appearance unless viewed under very strong light) with white enamel loops (*diam 3¾in   collection of Mr John Williams*).

Perhaps these were made from the dense ruby metal used for flashing sheet glass (see page 21).

97 *Below*: two case bottles in deep olive-green metal, with numerous air bubbles, kicks in bases and rough pontils (*height 11¾in, base 4 × 4in   collection of Mr John Williams*).

These items are not included as definitely being of Nailsea manufacture, but they were made by bottle houses in the eighteenth and nineteenth centuries, and a similar bottle is attributed to Nailsea in the specimens at Taunton Castle. It is quite likely that they were manufactured in the Bristol area, perhaps by one of the houses run by the Nailsea firm.

98   Toys in trailed clear glass, with enamel decoration (*collection of Mr John Williams*). *Left to right*: basket with blue rim and red bow on handle (*height 3½in*); candlestick and holder, blue frill and candle, red flame (*height 5in*); large teapot, treacle-brown spout and handle, and lid with deep blue frill (*height 4¼in*); small teapot, turquoise-blue spout and handle (*height 1½in*).

99   *Facing page*: cup and cover in pale green glass with a ribbed surface made in the late eighteenth or early nineteenth century (*height approx 9½in Victoria and Albert Museum, Buckley loan, ref 594 C 650 1936*).

100 Jug of dark transparent green metal decorated with white enamel
loops. Late eighteenth or early nineteenth century (*height 6¼in   Victoria and
Albert Museum, ref 573 1854*).

101 Jug of dark translucent yellowish-green metal, spirally streaked in white enamel. Late eighteenth or early nineteenth century (*Victoria and Albert Museum, ref 20 1911*).

102 Funnel of blue glass in the form of a bugle. Possibly a Bristol piece, about 1800 (*height 4¾in Victoria and Albert Museum*).

Such pieces are often attributed to Nailsea. Traditionally a product of the glassblower (see the bugle surmounting the 'ship' glass, of Netherlands manufacture, plate 116).

103   Jug in opaque white enamel glass with fragments of blue, green and red. Late eighteenth or early nineteenth century (*height 3in   Victoria and Albert Museum, ref C 643 1936*).

An interesting piece in so far as the white enamel so often used to decorate window and bottle glass with flecks and loops here forms the vessel itself, which is embedded with coloured fragments. Fine vessels were intentionally made in white enamel, some of them exquisitely decorated with bird and flower designs by Michael Edkins in Bristol, but the vessel illustrated looks like a typical 'incidental' piece made in the Nailsea tradition.

104 Pipe of clear glass decorated in opaque white, pink and blue. Early nineteenth century (*height 19½in   Victoria and Albert Museum, ref 196 1908*).

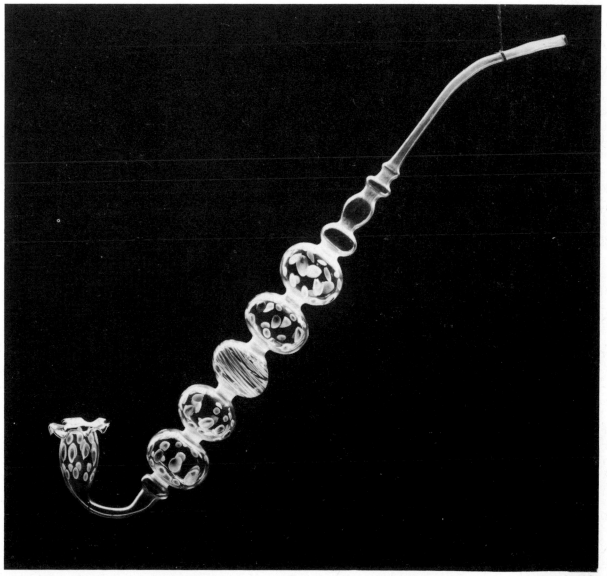

105   Three sixth-century BC Egyptian vessels (*Victoria and Albert Museum*).
Left: vase (*height 4½in*); *centre*: bottle (*5¼in*); *right*: jug (*4¾in*).

Although the method of making the vessel itself was different (molten glass
threads were wound round a sand core), it is worth noting the affinities
between the combed looped decoration and the forms of certain Egyptian and
Nailsea vessels. Note the threads round the rims of the vase and jug. The
looped decoration can be compared with the flasks in plates 45 and 79 and
the forms of the vase and bottle with the miniature scent bottles in plate 106
and the flask in plate 45. Further comparisons can of course be made elsewhere in the book.

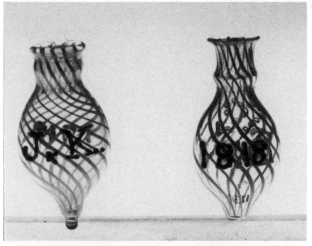

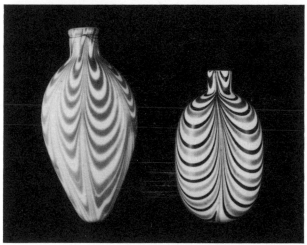

106 Miniature scent bottles in clear glass with white spiralled loops, dated and initialled (*actual height 1½in   Taunton Museum*).

Possibly made especially to order from the travelling glassmakers, as tokens of love (cf Egyptian vase and bottle, plate 105).

Flasks as·described (see plate 79; cf Egyptian vessels, plate 105) (*collection of Mr and Mrs S. J. Painter*). Flask as described (see plate 45; cf Egyptian vessels, plate 105) (*Taunton Museum*).

107 *Left*: early fragmented example of Near East crown glass, found at Jerash; *centre*: crown glass fragments *in situ* as found at Jerash; *right*: a modern example made at Hebron (*Science Museum, London*).

108 Two examples of Roman crown glass, of bowl shape (*Science Museum, London*).

109 Small bottle of Teutonic greenish glass with spiralled threads of the same metal round the body (cf plates 9 and 118 for use of same technique) (*Victoria and Albert Museum*).

110 Roman bowl of brownish glass with white loops and threads, first century AD (*height 2½in, diam 3in Victoria and Albert Museum, ref C 58 1966*).

111 Venetian late six-teenth- or early seventeenth-century vase with finely controlled combed looped (latticinio) decoration (*height 14in Victoria and Albert Museum, ref 5229 1901*).

Many comparisons can be made with Nailsea examples and with the Egyptian vessels illustrated in plate 105.

112　Two fine winged Venetian goblets with latticinio bowls. Perfection of the latticinio technique was achieved by the Venetians (*Victoria and Albert Museum, ref C 204–5 1936*).

113 *Facing page*: seventeenth-century Spanish ewer with combed latticinio decoration (*height 7in Victoria and Albert Museum, ref 93 1853*).

114 *Right*: seventeenth-century Spanish jug of blue and white mottled glass (*height 8½in Victoria and Albert Museum, ref 334 73*).

115 *Left*: French bottle of greyish-blue transparent glass, heavily splashed in various colours. Late sixteenth century (*height 8¾in Victoria and Albert Museum, ref 5268 1901*).

116 *Facing page*: 'Ship' glass from the Netherlands in the form of the hull of a ship with open-work rigging set on a high foot with a hollow fluted knop, surmounted by a bugle. Second half of the seventeenth century (*height 16¼in Victoria and Albert Museum, Buckley loan, ref C 506 1936*).

An aristocratic forebear of the type of English ship (see plate 86). Cf also the bugle in Bristol blue, plate 102.

117 English serving-jug in green bottle glass, sealed Philip Sergeant 1717 (*height 9in Victoria and Albert Museum, ref C 77 1947*).

The date of this vessel suggests an early diversification by an English bottle house.

118 English jug in green glass with spiral thread of the same metal around the rim, with blue and white combed latticinio or ribbed decoration. Made by James Powell & Sons, 1876 (*height 8½in Victoria and Albert Museum, ref 548 1877*).

A post-Nailsea piece which shows the influence of the decorative techniques used at Nailsea, Bristol and elsewhere, and the continuity back through different periods and cultures to the beginnings of the art and craft of glassmaking in Ancient Egypt.

BIBLIOGRAPHY

Buckland, Anna J. *The Life of Hannah More – A Lady of Two Centuries*. Religious Tract Society, 1885.

Buckley, Francis.'The Early Glasshouses of Bristol', *Transactions of the Society of Glass Technology*, Vol 9 (Sheffield, 1925).

Chance, Sir Hugh. 'The Nailsea Glassworks', *Pottery Gazette and Glass Trade Review* (January 1958).

——. 'Nailsea Glass', *Circle of Glass Collectors,* No 128 (1962).

——. 'The Nailsea Story', *Chance Comments* (magazine of Chance Bros Ltd), Vol 15, No 3 (August–September 1962).

——. 'Records and the Nailsea Glassworks', *The Connoisseur* (July 1967).

——. 'The Nailsea Glassworks', *Studies in Glass History and Design*, papers read to Committee B Sessions at the Eighth International Congress on Glass, London, July 1968, ed R. J. Charleston (Society of Glass Technology, University of Sheffield, 1968).

Chance, James Frederick. *A History of the Firm of Chance Brothers, Glass and Alkali Manufacturers* (Spottiswoode, Ballantyne, 1919).

Gray, H. St George.'Nailsea Glass', *The Connoisseur*, Vol 30 (June 1911).

——. 'Nailsea and Other Glass in the Collection of Mr John Lane and Margaret Lavington', *The Connoisseur,* Vol 57 (June 1920).

——. 'Notes on the Nailsea Glassworks', *The Connoisseur*, Vol 65 (1923).

Greenhill, B. J. 'The Story of the Nailsea Glassworks', *Clevedon Mercury* (21 June 1961).

McKearin, Helen and George S. *Two Hundred Years of American Blown Glass* (New York: Crown, 1946).

Watkins, Lura Woodside. *American Glass and Glassmaking* (New York: Parrish, 1950).

Glass History and *Making Glass*, published by the Glass Manufacturers Association, contain much useful general background information.

Unpublished manuscript sources:

Eyres, J. M., of Exeter, boy clerk at the Nailsea Works from 1862 to 1869. Autobiography.

Maxwell, H. W., one-time Director of the Bristol City Art Gallery. The Early Connections of the Glassworks at Nailsea and Bristol.

Mountain, Francis. History of the Nailsea Glassworks, written when seventy-two years of age, for the Bristol City Museum and Art Gallery, c1915.

Other material:

Bristol Gazette from 1788.

Children's Employment Commission, Evidence 1865, pp217–18.

C. T. Coathupe's Works Notebook for 1836.

J. M. Eyres's letter from 12 Powderham Crescent, Exeter, dated 10 July 1911, to H. St George Gray, Curator, Taunton Museum.

Bristol Presentments (Imports and Exports) edited by the Collector of Customs. Filed in Bristol Reference Library, covering period 1770–1917 (some gaps).

ACKNOWLEDGEMENTS

I am particularly indebted to Sir Hugh Chance who has shown warm interest in my project and who released to me relevant family correspondence and his own correspondence with the late H. St George Gray, one-time Curator of the Castle Museum, Taunton. I am grateful for his advice on a number of technical points and for the loan of photographs of historical and topographical interest and of his own collection of Nailsea glass. Sir Hugh, whose ancestors founded and developed the Nailsea glassworks, has done much valuable detailed and accurate research into the Nailsea story and the results of his work were of great help in the writing of this book. Sir Hugh has written a number of articles and papers on this subject and these are listed in the Bibliography.

I warmly thank everyone else who has given me assistance in the preparation of the book, including Mrs Patricia Elton and the National Trust at Clevedon Court for allowing me to photograph many items in its collection; Lady Elton of Clevedon Court; Miss C. N. Hasnip, Assistant Keeper at the Castle Museum, Taunton, for much patience and practical help during a number of visits to take photographs; Miss Cleo Witt, Curator of Applied Art at the Bristol City Art Gallery; Mary Williams, Bristol City Archivist and her assistant, John Williams; Miss A. J. Atkinson, Area Librarian at Nailsea, Bristol and the Assistant County Librarian, Bridgwater, for making references in their possession available; R. J. Charleston, Keeper of Ceramics, Victoria and Albert Museum for his interest and help; H. W. Maxwell, one-time Director of the Bristol City Art Gallery for the loan of his notes on the subject and copies of papers relating to the history of the Nailsea glassworks; Dwight P. Lamnon, Curator of European Glass, the Corning Museum of Glass, New York, and Emma N. Papert, Assistant Museum Librarian, Photograph and Slide Library, Metropolitan Museum of Art, New York, for their help regarding Nailsea glass in their respective museums' collections and affinities between Nailsea glass and certain kinds of American glass; Mr and Mrs S. J. Painter and Mr John Williams of Somerset who gave me hospitality, practical help with photographing and trust and patience in allowing me to handle their collections; and finally to my wife Miranda, without whose tacit support it would have been much more difficult a task to complete the book.

The plates in this volume are reproduced with thanks as follows:

Plates

1, 55–60	Items from the Bristol City Art Gallery, photographed by Derek Balmer, photographer, Bristol
2–5, 62–6	Kindly loaned by Sir Hugh Chance
6, 52–3, 107–8	Crown copyright, Science Museum, London
7–29	Photographed by the author by courtesy of Mrs P. Elton and the National Trust, at Clevedon Court
30–51, 54, 106	Photographed by the author by permission of the Castle Museum, Taunton
61	Photographed by the author by courtesy of Lady Elton, Clevedon Court
67–89	Photographed by the author by courtesy of Mr and Mrs S. J. Painter
90–8	Photographed by the author by courtesy of Mr John Williams
99–105, 109–18	Crown copyright, Victoria and Albert Museum

INDEX